Flamingo Watching

FLAMINGO WATCHING

Poems by
Kay Ryan

Copper Beech Press

for Carol

Grateful acknowledgment is made to the magazines in which some of these poems originally appeared:

American Poetry Review: "Every Painting by Chagall"
The American Scholar: "Les Natures Profondement Bonnes
    Sont Toujours Indecises"
Antioch Review: "Flamingo Watching"
The Atlantic: "Emptiness" and "This Life"
Epoch: "Poetry Is a Kind of Money"
The Formalist: "Spring"
G.W. Review: "Leaving Spaces"
Kenyon Review: "A Certain Meanness of Culture" and "The
    Tables Freed"
MSS: "The Hinge of Spring"
The New Republic: "The Palm at the End of the Mind" and
    "Turtle"
Paris Review: "Yellow"
Partisan Review: "Is It Modest?" and "Periphery"
TriQuarterly: "A Certain Kind of Eden" and "Glass Slippers"
Yale Review: "The Animal Itself"
ZYZZYVA: "Extraordinary Lengths," "Masterworks of Ming,"
    and "On the Primacy of Green"

The author wishes to thank the Marin Arts Council for its support.

For information, please write the publisher:
    Copper Beech Press
    Post Office Box 2578
    Providence, Rhode Island 02906

Library of Congress Cataloging-in-Publication Data
Ryan, Kay.
    Flamingo watching : poems / by Kay Ryan.
        p. cm.
    ISBN-10: 0-914278-64-9 (alk. pap. : pbk.) : $9.95
    ISBN-13: 978-0-914278-64-1
    I. Title.
    PS3568.Y38F57   1994
    811'.54—dc20   94-14755
                                                  CIP

Set in New Baskerville by Louis Giardini
Printed and bound by McNaughton & Gunn
Manufactured in the United States of America
Second Printing

CONTENTS

Part III: Common Names

Part One: Habitat and Range

FLAMINGO WATCHING

Wherever the flamingo goes,
she brings a city's worth
of furbelows. She seems
unnatural by nature —
too vivid and peculiar
a structure to be pretty,
and flexible to the point
of oddity. Perched on
those legs, anything she does
seems like an act. Descending
on her egg or draping her head
along her back, she's
too exact and sinuous
to convince an audience
she's serious. The natural elect,
they think, would be less pink,
less able to relax their necks,
less flamboyant in general.
They privately expect that it's some
poorly jointed bland grey animal
with mitts for hands
whom God protects.

THIS LIFE

It's a pickle, this life.
Even shut down to a trickle
it carries every kind of particle
that causes strife on a grander scale:
to be miniature is to be swallowed
by a miniature whale. Zeno knew
the law that we know: no matter
how carefully diminished, a race
can only be *half* finished with success;
then comes the endless halving of the rest —
the ribbon's stalled approach, the helpless
red-faced urgings of the coach.

EXTRAORDINARY LENGTHS

The only justification
for extraordinary lengths
is extraordinary distances.
Yet you don't find this
in the majority of instances.
No, rather you see lengths
swagged from balconies,
ribbons of lengths rippling
languidly, lengths spooling
from enchanted cavities and
grots. Actually there is
hardly a spot of sky or pool
of water uncolored by some
extraordinary length or other.
Brothers fling bolts of gossamer
off buildings with spectacular
results. Birds negotiate an
aerial spaghetti, surefooted
goats find themselves unsteady.
Poor people in brightly
lacquered boats just help
themselves to lengths
that tangle up and float
as pleasantly as kelp.

ON THE PRIMACY OF GREEN

Green was the first color
to get out of the water,
leaving the latter blue
and preceding yellow
which had to follow
because of fall.
We all know
about fall and how
chlorophyll shuts down
like a town under snow.
Returning to green,
moss in the rain
is the greenest
of greens seen
off the backs of lizards,
and is preferred
for its wider range
of occurrence.
It outlines bricks
like an artist, blankets
stumps, announces North,
beards rocks. It is useless
to enumerate its works.
The number of possible
green digits is infinite.
Green can be breathed.
The blind cannot be
deceived by imitations.
They smell when a chameleon
starts easing red up its tail:
vermillion smells Christian,
which is not to say unpleasant,
but so *fraught;* whereas
emeralds and chartreuses
are not. We associate

freedom with garden
and garden with Eden,
which is the word for green
in Precambrian.
By Adam's time
it had narrowed to a
certain shade of lime
favored for bowers and
serpents, being a color
somehow both restful and
urgent. But anyhow
by then the whole rainbow
was becoming more seductive
than available.

YELLOW

Yellow is the most
primary of the colors,
owing nothing to any
of the others. Many
descendants come back
repentant and sullied
to celebrate yellow's
anniversary, but yellow
is unapproachable, not
antisocial but not
interested in sitting
at the table with
tainted yolks or
nouveaux chartreuses
or any of the other
abuses of the palette.
Yellow's indifferent
to blue's inducements
and despises orange,
red's bastard coinage.
He's selfish, yes you
could say he's selfish;
but it's Spring's wish,
just at this brief first note
before her fantasia,
to soft-petal every shade
but acacia.

EVERY PAINTING BY CHAGALL

Every twined groom and bride,
every air fish, smudged Russian,
red horse, yellow chicken, assumes
its position not actually beside
but in some friendly distribution
with a predictable companion.
Every canvas insists on a
similar looseness, each neck
put to at least two uses. And wings
from some bottomless wing source.
They are pleasure wings of course
since any horse or violinist
may mount the blue
simply by wanting to.
(In freedom, dear things
repeat without tedium.)

THE TABLES FREED

*The presence of real objects is a nightmare for me.
I have always overturned objects. A chair or table
turned upside down gives me peace and satisfaction.*
                                        Chagall

A companionable flood can
make things wobble. The
sober table at last enjoys
the bubbles locked in her
grain, straining together
good as Egyptians to shift
the predictable plane.
Dense plates and books
slide off and dive or bloat
but she floats, a legged
boat nosing the helpless
stationaries, the bolted
basin, the metal reliquaries —
in short, the nouns. All over
town tables are bumping
out of doors, negotiating
streets and beginning to
meet at water corners
like packs of mustangs,
blue, red, yellow, stencilled,
enlivened by swells as
wild horses are stretched
liquid and elegant by hills.

LEAVING SPACES

It takes a courageous
person to leave spaces
empty. Certainly any
artist in the Middle Ages
felt this timor, and quickly
covered space over
with griffins, sea serpents,
herbs and brilliant carpets
of flowers — things pleasant
or unpleasant, no matter.
Of course they were cowards
and patronized by cowards
who liked their swards as
filled with birds as leaves.
All of them believed in
sudden edges and completely
barren patches in the mind,
and they didn't want to
think about them all the time.

PERIPHERY

Unlike igneous
crystal-studded
porphyry, famous
since the Egyptian
basin business,
periphery is no
one substance,
but the edges
of anything.
Fountains, for instance,
have a periphery
at some distance
from the spray.
On nice days
idle people circle
all the way around
the central spout.
They do not get wet.
They do not get hot.
If they bring a bottle
they get kicked out, but
generally things are mild
and tolerant at peripheries.
People bring bread the
pigeons eat greedily.

THE MOCK RUIN

> *... built as the backdrop of the stage of the ancient*
> *Roman theatre in Sabratha, Libya, Africa, is the most*
> *perfectly preserved part of the entire structure.*
> Ripley's *Believe It or Not!*

Fakes and mockups, stage backdrops
quickly nicked, weathered, and
stuck together for illusion's sake
(getting some parts backwards)
give more, maybe; sway slightly;
take later buffets better generally
than their brittle sources whose
stones were set down in regular courses
and mortared. Maybe there is something
to falseness that doesn't get reported.

IS IT MODEST?

Is it modest or arrogant
not to enter the scene;
instead to push a parrot
forward or make the air
apparent in the spring;
to press the whole embarrassment
of riches at us, bejeweling
every mean web, glazing
water in ditches; to divest
yourself upon us till
every moth or hibiscus
or bottle fragment is some
aspect of your garment,
some hem to kiss; un-becoming
on and on, leaving us like this?

THE THINGS OF THE WORLD

Wherever the eye lingers
it finds a hunger.
The things of the world
want us for dinner.
Inside each pebble or leaf
or puddle is a hook.
The appetites of the world
compete to catch a look.
What does this mean
and how does it work?
Why aren't rocks complete?
Why isn't green adequate
to green? We aren't gods
whose gaze could save,
but that's how the things
of the world behave.

EMPTINESS

Emptiness cannot be
compressed. Nor can it
fight abuse. Nor is there
an endless West hosting
elk, antelope, and the
tough cayuse. This is
true also of the mind:
it can get used.

SLANT

Can or can't you feel
a dominant handedness
behind the randomness
of loss? Does a skew
insinuate into the
visual plane; do
the avenues begin to
strain for the diagonal?
Maybe there is always
this lean, this slight
slant. Maybe always
a little pressure
on the same rein,
a bias cut to everything,
a certain cant
it's better not to name.

APOLOGY

for E. B.

I thought you were
born to privilege,
some inherited advantage —
like an estate framed
in privet hedge,
or a better-feathered
shuttlecock for badinage,
or other French pretensions.
I never thought you knew about exhaustion —
how we have to leap in the morning
as early as high as possible,
we are so fastened, we are so dutiful.

VACATION

It would be pleasant to walk
in Stonehenge or other places
that have rocks arranged on the
basis of a plan, or plans,
inscrutable to modern man;
to wander among grinders
sunk deep in sheep pastures
or simply set on top Peruvian grit;
to gaze up at incisors
no conceivable jaw could fit;
to stretch to be ignorant enough,
scoured to a clean vessel
as pure as the puzzle, vestal
to a mystery involving people,
but without the heat of people.

A CERTAIN KIND OF EDEN

It seems like you could, but
you can't go back and pull
the roots and runners and replant.
It's all too deep for that.
You've overprized intention,
have mistaken any bent you're given
for control. You thought you chose
the bean and chose the soil.
You even thought you abandoned
one or two gardens. But those things
keep growing where we put them —
if we put them at all.
A certain kind of Eden holds us thrall.
Even the one vine that tendrils out alone
in time turns on its own impulse,
twisting back down its upward course
a strong and then a stronger rope,
the greenest saddest strongest
kind of hope.

Part II: Behavior

NO REST FOR THE IDLE

The idle are shackled
to their oars. The waters
of idleness are borderless
of course and must always
be plied. Relief is foreign
on this wide and featureless
ocean. There are no details:
no shores, no tides, no times
when things lift up and then
subside, no sails or smokestacks,
no gravel gathered up and spit back,
no plangencies, no sea birds startled;
the weather, without the Matthew Arnold.

THE NARROW PATH

*One can perhaps please one's self and earn that
slender right to persevere.*
                                        Marianne Moore

No rime-grizzled mountain climber,
puzzled by where to put his fingers next,
knows the least thing about
how narrow work gets
that depends only on pleasure.
When it gets late or he gets depressed,
he can hang in a nylon sack,
his whole weight waiting
for the light to come back.
But for people who ascend
only by pleasure
there are no holding straps.
They must keep to the
hairline crack all the time
or fall all the way back.

WHEN FISHING FAILS

*"Your husband is very lucky," observed Smithers, "to
have ornithology to fall back upon when fishing fails."*
Cyril Hare, *Death Is No Sportsman*

When fishing fails, when no bait avails,
and nothing speaks in liquid hints
of where the fishes went for weeks,
and dimpled ponds and silver creeks
go flat and tarnish, it's nice if
you can finish up your sandwich,
pack your thermos, and ford
this small hiatus toward
a second mild and absorbing purpose.

GLASS SLIPPERS

Despite the hard luck
of the ugly step sisters,
most people's feet will fit
into glass slippers.
The arch rises, the heel
tapers, the toes align
in descending order
and the whole thing slides
without talcum powder
into the test slipper.
We *can* shape to the
dreams of another; we are
eager to yield. It is a
mutual pleasure to the holder
of the slipper and to the
foot held. It is a singular
moment — tender, improbable,
and as yet unclouded by the
problems that hobble the pair
when they discover that
the matching slipper
isn't anywhere, nor does
the bare foot even share
the shape of the other.
When they compare,
the slippered foot makes
the other odder: it looks
like a hoof. So many miracles
don't start far back enough.

SAY IT STRAIGHT

I have a mania for straight writing — however circuitous I may be in what I myself say.
Marianne Moore

What we would
and what we can say
stray as in a dream;
a certain mad rectitude
creeps in, by which
something simple as an apple
can never be determined
wholly edible.
The crisp act is deferred,
the object blurred by scruples.
The more we cherish clarity
in principle, the more it is
impossible. Will enamel
ever strike the fruit?
Will Eve grow wild and forgivable?
For it's unlovable
to talk too long with snakes,
whose reasons fork
the more the more
she hesitates.

HOW SUCCESSFUL CAN SHE AFFORD TO BE?

Maybe the mime's test
would be to get you to drink
from the glass she passed.

What if you did
grasp it just right;
what if it did flash
in the window light?

Would she be glad
if it left a ring,
if she could
add to the manifest,
passing a thing
out of the dream?

How close to the door
can she lean,
how genuinely bid you enter,
where she herself is a guest
on her best behavior?

REPETITION

First the mind does something
to see if it can.
Then the mind does the same thing
because it can.
But there is mind left over:
the excited part.
This is the poison in repetition.
But it is a very weak poison
and no reason to forego
the deep abiding consolations
of repetition. The poison
may build up usefully,
as it built up in the Egyptians—
a preservative. What will ever
equal accretion's extravagance?
Take the grand conservative temples
to the golden Horus-headed pharaohs,
for instance.

LES NATURES PROFONDEMENT BONNES
SONT TOUJOURS INDECISES

One strong squirt
of will and the world
fills with direction.
All roads go Roman.
The path not taken
is not kept open.
There is suddenly
a rational waterworks
system. Things are done
as no indecisive person
could do them. Still
there is a population
that likes mistakes and
indecision, guarding
atavisms and anatomical
sports, the hips of snakes,
the wings of the horse.
They do not argue that
this is useful. They
make no mention of the
gene pool. They just
like to think about
these things. They
make them comfortable.

SO DIFFERENT

A tree is lightly connected
to its blossoms.
For a tree it is
a pleasant sensation
to be stripped
of what's white and winsome.
If a big wind comes,
any nascent interest in fruit
scatters. This is so different
from humans, for whom
what is un-set matters
so oddly — as though
only what is lost held possibility.

THE ANIMAL ITSELF

As to its digestion,
it digesteth very little.
It is an inefficient animal.
It goes through draft
on draft and is not slaked
of first thirst. Oh, to hear
its curse at its own pipes
would frighten a plumber.
The fittings it rigs, the long
lengths it extends till it is
a hollow giant angered
at the smallness of things —
all for the sake of the
small food it cannot bring in.
Stranded, it would have you understand;
its hunger-pain far as the toe
from the brain. How can it
help itself? It grows
daily more clumsy, builds
room on room and loses its family.
Oh, it is lonely. There should
be a patience born in those who
must eat infrequently, it thinks,
a sphinxlike willingness
to squat on one's own feet
and survey the blank expanse,
a comfort for the comfortless.
There should be a patience,
a lionlike somnolence.
Let me lie down and stretch
beneath the impartial sun,
warmed like any stone; let want
sleep deep within me, roused
and right-sized at opportunity —
the meanest flower that blows
could nourish me.

HALF A LOAF

The whole loaf's loft
is halved in profile,
like the standing side
of a bombed cathedral.

The cut face
of half a loaf
puckers a little.

The bread cells
are open and brittle
like touching coral.

It is nothing like the middle
of an uncut loaf,
nothing like a conceptual half
which stays moist.

I say do not adjust to half
unless you must.

SOFT

In harmony with the rule of irony —
which requires that we harbor the enemy
on this side of the barricade — the shell
of the unborn eagle or pelican, which is made
to give protection till the great beaks can harden,
is the first thing to take up poison.
The mineral case is soft and gibbous
as the moon in a lake — an elastic,
rubbery, nightmare water that won't break.
Elsewhere, also, I see the mockeries of struggle,
a softness over people.

SPRING

Winter, like a set opinion,
is routed. What gets it out?
The imposition of some external season,
or some internal doubt?
I see the yellow maculations spread
across bleak hills of what I said
I'd always think; a stippling of white
upon the grey; a pink the shade
of what I said I'd never say.

"I MARVELLED AT HOW GENERALLY I WAS AIDED"

(The Autobiography of Charles Darwin)

I marvel at how generally
I am aided, how frequently
the availability of help
is demonstrated. I've had
unbridgeable distances collapse
and opposite objects coalesce
enough to think duress itself
may be a prayer. Perhaps not chance,
but need, selects; and desperation
works upon giraffes until their necks
can reach the necessary branch.
If so, help alters; makes seven vertebrae
go farther in the living generation;
help coming to us, not from the fathers,
not to the children.

IMPERSONAL

The working Kabbalist
resists the lure of
the personal. She
suspends interest
in the Biblical list
of interdicted shell fish,
say, in order to
read the text another way.
It might seem to some
superficial to convert
letters to numerals
or in general refuse plot
in favor of dots or half circles;
it might easily seem
comical, how she
ignores an obviously
erotic tale except for
every third word,
rising for her like braille
for something vivid
as only the impersonal
can be — a crescent
bright as the moon,
a glimpse of a symmetry,
a message so vast
in its passage that
she must be utterly open
to an alien idea of person.

A CERTAIN MEANNESS OF CULTURE

> *And about Blake's supernatural territories, as about the supposed ideas that dwell there, we cannot help commenting on a certain meanness of culture. They illustrate the crankiness, the eccentricity, which frequently affects writers outside of the Latin tradition.*
>
> T.S. Eliot

What else can we do,
born on deserts
occupied haphazard
by borax traders
aspiring to a
stucco elegance
if they're real lucky?
Someone has to get here
before the mythology,
to be happy in the
first tailings of industry,
and of course lonely
and susceptible to
the opinions of donkeys
since donkeys are the
main company out here
among the claims.
Snakes and wild things
skitter off too fast
for conversation.
You can get an appreciation
for why a donkey is
fussy about books
since she carries them.
You start to value culture
like you would water.
I'd say this one's about

a two-cupper. And when
you dream, it's not romance.
Things are too thin
out here already to chance
sad endings. You get
pretty stringy and impatient
with the fat smoke off
old cities. You get cranky
and admire just what stands up
to the stars' cold and the
sun's fire. You like winches
and pulleys, picks and khakis,
and the rare sweet grass you can
find for your donkey.

THE TEST WE SET OURSELF

An honest work generates its own power; a
dishonest work tries to rob power from the
cataracts of the given.

Annie Dillard

If we could be less human,
if we could stand out of the range
of the cataracts of the given,
and not find our pockets swollen
with change we haven't — but must have —
stolen, who wouldn't?
It isn't a gift; we are beholden
to the sources we crib —
always something's overflow,
or someone's rib hidden in our breast;
the answer sewn inside us
that invalidates the test we set ourself
against the boneless angel at our right
and at our left the elf.

FORCE

Nothing forced works.
The Gordian knot just worsens
if it's jerked at by a person.
One of the main stations
of the cross is patience.
Another, of course, is impatience.
There is such a thing as
too much tolerance
for unpleasant situations,
a time when the gentle
teasing out of threads
ceases to be pleasing
to a woman born for conquest.
Instead she must assault
the knot or alp or everest
with something sharp,
and take upon herself
the moral warp of sudden progress.

Part III: Common Names

MINERS' CANARIES

It isn't arbitrary;
it isn't curious;
miners' canaries
serve ordinary purposes
with just a fillip of
extra irony.
Something is always
testing the edges
of the breathable —
not so sweet, not so yellow,
but something is always
living at the wrong edge
of the arable; something
is always excused first
from the water table,
chalking the boundary
of the possible
from the far side;
even in the individual.

THE HINGE OF SPRING

The jackrabbit is a mild herbivore
grazing the desert floor,
quietly abridging spring,
eating the color off everything
rampant-height or lower.

Rabbits are one of the things
coyotes are for. One quick scream,
a few quick thumps,
and a whole little area
shoots up blue and orange clumps.

DEER

To lure a single swivel ear,
one tentative twig of a leg,
or a nervous tail here,
is to mark this place
as the emperor's park,
rife, I say rife, with deer.
For if one leaf against the littered floor
be cleft with the true arc,
all this lost ground, and more,
becomes a park. Everywhere
the nearest deer signals the nearest dark.
A buck looks up: the touch of his rack
against wet bark whispers a syllable
singular to deer; the next one hears
and shifts; the next head stops
and lifts; deeper and deeper into the park.

SHEEP IN WOLVES' CLOTHING

Of all the unpleasant
affectations of *soi disant*
wolves, the most unpleasant
is their teeth: blunt ruminant
sheep stumps built up
to something no one could
really kill with. Decorative
in the worst sense. An offense
to economy and outright
blasphemy in the context
of true wolf philosophy,
which states very clearly
that every bluff must
promote good. Which means
you eat what you've fooled:
all of Little Red Riding,
from her shoes to her hood.

SNAKE CHARM

Oh for even a fingerling snake,
a three-inch inspiration full of
genetic information about length,
the making of venom, and the start
of muscles later on used for compression.
A snake, say, in a Moorish pattern, abstract,
ornamental, repeatable over a whole Toledo
without tedium. Yes, a snake the sun stretches,
a snake that improves everything it catches:
the adventitious mouse converted to stripes
or diamond patches. This snake is reckless,
with no concern for balance. It can
slide over any surface, a silent line,
an endless pattern, a generative rhyme.

THE PALM AT THE END OF THE MIND

After fulfilling everything
one two three he came back again
free, no more prophecy requiring
that he enter the city just this way,
no more set-up treacheries.
It was the day after Easter. He adored
the egg-shell litter and the cellophane
caught in the grass. Each door he passed
swung with its own business, all the
witnesses along his route of pain
again distracted by fear of loss
or hope of gain. It was wonderful
to be a man, bewildered by
so many flowers, the rush
and ebb of hours, his own
ambiguous gestures — his
whole heart exposed, then
taking cover.

POETRY IS A KIND OF MONEY

Poetry is a kind of money
whose value depends upon reserves.
It's not the paper it's written on
or its self-announced denomination,
but the bullion, sweated from the earth
and hidden, which preserves its worth.
Nobody knows how this works,
and how can it? Why does something
stacked in some secret bank or cabinet,
some miser's trove, far back, lambent,
and gloated over by its golem, make us
so solemnly convinced of the transaction
when Mandelstam says *love,* even
in translation?

MASTERWORKS OF MING

Ming, Ming,
such a lovely
thing blue
and white

bowls and
basins glow
in museum
light

they would
be lovely
filled with
rice or
water

so nice
adjunct
to dinner

or washing
a daughter

a small
daughter
of course
since it's
a small basin

first you
would put
one then

the other
end in

PERSIFLAGE

Garden serpents
small as shoe laces
are found in
side lots and
grassy places.
Green coat
striped with yellow
makes the garden viper
a dapper fellow.
Birds mock
and children chase
our minor adder
thinner than a pencil.
Born sans puff or rattle
he counts on persiflage
in battle. Before
his flippant tongue
children stiffen,
dogs fall like
beef cattle.

BREAST BIRDS

Breast birds don't breed true.
Once you let them out of you
their vividness is brief;
their pink or blue
fades back to brown
as quick as your relief.
Oh love, oh loneliness, oh grief.

PAIRED THINGS

Who, who had only seen wings,
could extrapolate the
skinny sticks of things
birds use for land,
the backward way they bend,
the silly way they stand?
And who, only studying
birdtracks in the sand,
could think those little forks
had decamped on the wind?
So many paired things seem odd.
Who ever would have dreamed
the broad winged raven of despair
would quit the air and go
bandylegged upon the ground,
a common crow?

OSPREY

The great taloned osprey
nests in Scotland.
Her nest's the biggest
thing around, a spiked basket
with hungry ugly osprey offspring
in it. For months she sits on it.
He fishes, riding two-pound salmon
home like rockets. They get
all the way there before they die,
so muscular and brilliant
swimming through the sky.

TURTLE

Who would be a turtle who could help it?
A barely mobile hard roll, a four-oared helmet,
she can ill afford the chances she must take
in rowing toward the grasses that she eats.
Her track is graceless, like dragging
a packing-case places, and almost any slope
defeats her modest hopes. Even being practical,
she's often stuck up to the axle on her way
to something edible. With everything optimal,
she skirts the ditch which would convert
her shell into a serving dish. She lives
below luck-level, never imagining some lottery
will change her load of pottery to wings.
Her only levity is patience,
the sport of truly chastened things.